To:

_____

From:

_____

Date:

_____

Whatever you ask for in prayer, believe that
you have received it, and it will be yours.

—*Mark 11:24*

Prayer Through the Eyes of Women of the Bible
Copyright 2000 by Ann Spangler and Jean E. Syswerda
ISBN 0-310-98415-7

Adapted from *Women of the Bible* by Ann Spangler and Jean E.
Syswerda © 1999 by Ann Spangler and Jean E. Syswerda (Grand
Rapids, MI: Zondervan Publishing House, 1999).

Requests for information should be addressed to:
    Inspirio, the Gift Group of Zondervan
    Grand Rapids, Michigan 49530
    http://www.inspiriogifts.com

Design Manager & Interior design: Amy E. Langeler
Associate Editor: Molly C. Detweiler
Assistant Editor: Heidi Carvella
Cover design: Tammy Johnson, Flat River Graphics

Printed in China
02 03 04 /HK/ 4

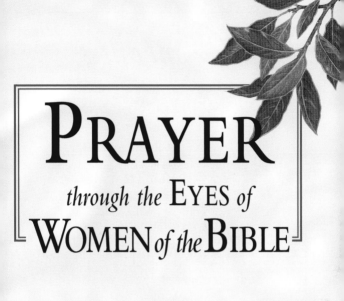

PRAYER
through the EYES of
WOMEN of the BIBLE

ANN SPANGLER &
JEAN E. SYSWERDA

inspirio
The gift group of Zondervan

Contents

To Judy Weaver
Your faith has strengthened mine
—Ann Spangler

To my daughters, Holly and Shelly
You have shown me the beauty of
young women of God
—Jean E. Syswerda

Though the narratives in this book at times rely on fictional techniques to bring out various dimensions of a story and the character's emotional responses, every effort has been made to remain close to the original text, drawing out reasonable implications from Scripture's account.

Which means

"chieftainess" or

"princess."

The name of Abram's wife was Sarai ... Now Sarai was barren; she had no children. ...

God said to Abraham, "As for Sarai your wife, you are no longer to call her Sarai; her name will be Sarah. I will bless her and will surely give you a son by her. I will bless her so that she will be the mother of nations." ...

Sarah became pregnant and bore a son to Abraham in his old age, at the very time God had promised him. ... Sarah said, "God has brought me laughter, and everyone who hears about this will laugh with me." And she added, "Who would have said to Abraham that Sarah would nurse children? Yet I have borne him a son in his old age."

Genesis 11:29–30; 17:15–16; 21:2, 6–7

Her Character

Beautiful enough to attract rulers in the ancient world, Sarah could be strong-willed and jealous. Yet she was considered a loyal wife who did what was right and didn't give in to fear.

Her Sorrow

That she remained childless for most of her life.

Her Joy

That at the age of ninety, she gave birth to Isaac, child of the promise.

Sarah was sixty-five when she began a journey that would lead her into uncharted spiritual territory. She and her husband Abraham moved miles south to Canaan, a land fertile with the promises of God but barren of everything cherished and familiar. God had promised the land to Abraham and his offspring. From him would come an entire nation.

If Abraham was to father a new nation, surely Sarah would be its mother. Yet she longed to give birth, not to a nation, but to one small child she could kiss and cradle.

Years passed and still there was no child. So Sarah took matters into her own hands. Following a practice common in the ancient world, she asked Abraham to sleep with her Egyptian maid. Hagar would become a surrogate mother for the promised child. Before long Ishmael was born, and peace vanished between the two women.

Later the Lord appeared to Abraham and said, "Sarah herself will have a son."

Now Sarah, eavesdropping from inside the tent, laughed in disbelief and said, "Now that I am old, will I still have this pleasure?"

But a year later Sarah gave birth to Isaac, whose name meant "laughter." Of course, the joke was not lost on the ninety-year-old mother, who exclaimed: "God has brought me laughter, and everyone who hears about this will laugh with me."

Was Sarah ashamed, perhaps years later, of her harsh treatment of Hagar and Ishmael? Did she regret laughing when God told Abraham she would bear a child at the age of ninety? Did she appreciate the echoing irony in young Isaac's laughter? Did she have any idea she would one day be revered as the Mother of Israel? Scripture does not say. But it is heartening to realize that God accomplishes his purposes despite our frailties, our small faith, our entrenched self-reliance. Despite her skepticism about God's ability to keep his promises, Sarah was a risk-taker of the first order, a woman who said goodbye to everything familiar in order to live an adventure that began with a promise and ended with laughter.

By faith Abraham, even though he was past age—and Sarah herself was barren—was enabled to become a father because he considered him faithful who had made the promise. And so from this one man, and he as good as dead, came descendants as numerous as the stars in the sky and as countless as the sand on the seashore.

Against all hope, Abraham in hope believed and so became the father of many nations, just as it had been said to him, "So shall your offspring be." Without weakening in his faith, he faced the fact that his body was as good as dead—since he was about a hundred years old—and that Sarah's womb was also dead. Yet he did not waver through unbelief regarding the promise of God, but was strengthened in his faith and gave glory to God, being fully persuaded that God had power to do what he had promised.

HEBREWS 11:11–12, ROMANS 4:18–21

Sarah's dream was to give birth to a son. God hints at his purpose for you by planting dreams within your heart. Find a quiet place and spend some time focusing on your dreams. Ask yourself what dreams you've been too busy, too afraid, or too disappointed to pursue. Write them down and pray about each one. If you take the plunge, you might find yourself joyfully echoing Sarah's words in Genesis 21:6: "God has brought me laughter."

Father, thank you for loving me despite the fact that my soul still contains shadows that sometimes block the light of your Spirit. As I grow older, may I trust you more completely for the dreams you've implanted in my soul and for the promises you've made to me. May I be surrounded by laughter at the wonderful way you accomplish your purpose despite my weakness.

Hagar

Her name is

Egyptian and may

mean either

"fugitive" or

"immigrant."

After Abram had been living in Canaan ten years, Sarai his wife took her Egyptian maidservant Hagar and gave her to her husband to be his wife. He slept with Hagar, and she conceived. … So Hagar bore Abram a son. …

Abraham took some food and a skin of water and gave them to Hagar. … She went on her way and wandered in the desert. … When the water in the skin was gone, she put the boy under one of the bushes. Then she went off and sat down nearby, about a bowshot away, for she thought, "I cannot watch the boy die." And as she sat there nearby, she began to sob … and the angel of God called to Hagar from heaven and said to her, "What is the matter, Hagar? Do not be afraid; God has heard the boy crying as he lies there. Lift the boy up and take him by the hand, for I will make him into a great nation."

GENESIS 16:3–4, 15; 21:14–18

Her Character

A foreigner and slave, she let pride overtake her when she bore Abraham a son. A woman with few resources, she suffered harshly for her mistake. She obeyed God's voice as soon as she heard it and was given a promise that her son would father a great nation.

Her Sorrow

That she was taken from her homeland to become a slave in a foreign land.

Her Joy

To know that God saw her suffering and heard her cry and that he helped her when she needed him most.

An Egyptian slave and Sarah's bitter rival, Hagar still had one thing that her mistress never enjoyed—a personal revelation of God. It happened when she was alone and afraid, without a shekel to her name—but that's getting ahead of the story.

Of the three parties involved in the scheme to make Hagar a surrogate mother, she was perhaps the only innocent one, a slave with little power to resist. But as soon as she discovered her pregnancy, Hagar began lording it over her mistress.

Sarah retaliated by making life so difficult that Hagar ran away into the desert. She hadn't gotten far before she heard a voice calling, "Hagar, maid of Sarah, go back to your mistress and submit to her." Then, as if to sweeten the order, came a word of assurance: "You are now pregnant and will bear a son; name him Ishmael, for the Lord has seen how miserable you are."

God's word had found her in the wilderness. He had seen her bondage, her bitterness, her anxiety about the future.

He knew about the child in her womb, naming him, "Ishmael," meaning

"God hears." In the future, every time Hagar would hold her son close, watch him play, or worry about his future, she would remember that God was near. It must have been assurance enough, for she returned to her mistress as God commanded.

Some sixteen years later, Hagar found herself once again in the wilderness. Sarah had finally expelled her and Ishmael from their home. Nearing death, Hagar placed her son under a bush and withdrew, unable to witness his agony.

Her weeping was soon broken by an angel's voice, "Do not be afraid; God has heard the boy crying as he lies there. Take him by the hand, for I will make him into a great nation." With that, the angel revealed a well of water that would save her son's life.

The last we see of Hagar, she is living in the desert, busy about the task of securing a wife, and therefore a future, for Ishmael. God had made a way in the wilderness for a single woman and her son, without friends, family, or resources to help her. He had seen, he had heard, he had indeed been faithful.

Know that the LORD has set apart
the godly for himself;
   the LORD will hear when I call to
   him.

PSALM 4:3

In my distress I called to the LORD;
   I cried to my God for help.
From his temple he heard my voice;
   my cry came before him, into his ears.

PSALM 18:6

Do not be anxious about anything,
but in everything, by prayer and petition, with thanksgiving, present your
requests to God. And the peace of God,
which transcends all understanding, will
guard your hearts and your minds in
Christ Jesus.

PHILIPPIANS 4:6–7

Invite a couple of close friends to join you for a Middle Eastern meal of olives, figs, pita bread, nuts, humus and tabbouleh (a salad made with cracked wheat, tomatoes, parsley, mint, onions, lemon juice, and olive oil) and then pray a special grace thanking God for providing so richly even when you felt you were living through a desert season in your life. Share stories with each other about how God has provided even when you weren't sure he was listening to your prayers.

Lord, sometimes I feel abandoned, as though no one understands or cares about me. Please show me that you really are near and that you see and hear everything that happens. Refresh me with your presence even when I am walking through a desert experience. And help me, in turn, to comfort others when they feel hopeless and alone.

Which means

"ewe."

Rachel was lovely in form, and beautiful. Jacob was in love with Rachel and said [to her father Laban], "I'll work for you seven years in return for your younger daughter Rachel." ...

Laban gave [Jacob] his daughter Rachel to be his wife. ...

When Rachel saw that she was not bearing Jacob any children ... she said to Jacob, "Give me children, or I'll die!" ...

Then God remembered Rachel. ... She became pregnant and gave birth to a son and ... named him Joseph, and said "May the LORD add to me another son."

Rachel began to give birth and had great difficulty. ... As she breathed her last—for she was dying—she named her son Ben-Oni. But his father named him Benjamin.

GENESIS 29:17–18; 29:28; 30:1;
30:22–24; 35:16, 18

Her Character

Manipulated by her father, she had little control over her circumstances and relationships. But rather than dealing creatively with a difficult situation, she behaved like a victim who responded to sin with yet more sin, making things worse by competing with her sister.

Her Sorrow

That her rivalry with her sister, Leah, spread to their children.

Her Joy

That her husband cherished her and would do whatever was in his power to make her happy.

"Was it better to have Jacob's love or to bear his children? Why did she even have to make such a choice?" The question battered Rachel, like wind slamming the same door again and again.

Years earlier, Rachel's father, Laban, had betrothed her to his nephew, Jacob, with the condition that the young man work for him for seven years. But when her wedding day arrived, Laban disguised Leah in Rachel's wedding garments. After dark he led Leah, covered by a veil, to Jacob's tent. As the first light crept across the tent floor, Jacob reached for Rachel only to find Leah at his side.

But soon Laban struck another bargain with Jacob, giving him Rachel in exchange for seven more years of labor. So the two sisters lived uneasily together, Leah's sons a grating reminder that Rachel, the second wife, was cheated still.

"Give me children or I'll die," she screamed at Jacob one day—as though he were God, able to create life.

Finally Rachel gave birth to a son, naming him Joseph, meaning "may he add"—a prophetic prayer that God would add yet another child to her line.

One day God told Jacob to return to the land of his fathers. More than twenty years before, Jacob had wrestled the family blessing from Esau and had fled from his anger. As Jacob and his family made their way across the desert, Jacob faced his brother and the two reconciled.

Soon after, Rachel struggled to give birth to a second son, the answer to her many prayers. Ironically, the woman who once said she would die unless she had children actually died giving birth.

Like her husband, the beautiful Rachel had been both schemer and victim. Tricked by her own father, she viewed her children as weapons in the struggle with her sister. Yet through a remarkable set of twists and turns, Rachel's Joseph would one day rule Egypt, providing a refuge for his father and brothers in the midst of famine. Using people with mixed motives and confused desires (the only kind of people there are), God would once again reveal his grace and mercy.

~

You understand, O LORD;
remember me and care for me.

JEREMIAH 15:15

Praise the LORD.
How good it is to sing praises
to our God,
*   how pleasant and fitting to praise*
him! ...
He heals the brokenhearted
*   and binds up their wounds. ...*
Great is our Lord
*   and mighty in power;*
*   his understanding has no limit.*

PSALM 147:1, 3, 5

Like Rachel, many of us tend to view other women as competition rather than as potential friends and sisters. Examine your own relationships and ask God to help you develop deep and satisfying relationships with other women. Then think of one woman you would like to get to know better. Call her! One expert says it takes an average of three years to form a solid friendship. Don't waste another moment!

Father, forgive me for letting my identity rest on whose wife or mother I am or what kind of job I have. I don't want to view other women as my rivals but as potential friends and even soulmates. Please lead me to the friendships I desire and help me to be patient with the process.

Which may mean

"impatient" or

"wild cow."

Now Laban had two daughters; the name of the older was Leah, and the name of the younger was Rachel. Leah had weak eyes, but Rachel was lovely in form, and beautiful. Jacob was in love with Rachel. ...

When evening came, [Laban] took his daughter Leah and gave her to Jacob, and Jacob lay with her. ...When morning came, there was Leah! So Jacob said to Laban, "What is this you have done to me? I served you for Rachel, didn't I? Why have you deceived me?" ...

When the Lord saw that Leah was not loved, he opened her womb, but Rachel was barren.

GENESIS 29:16–18, 23, 25, 31

Her Character

Capable of both strong and enduring love, she was a faithful mother and wife. Manipulated by her father, she battled with her sister for their husband's love and attention.

―⁓―

Her Sorrow

That she lacked her sister's beauty and that her love for her husband was one-sided.

―⁓―

Her Joy

That she bore Jacob six sons and one daughter.

"We buried Rachel today. But she is still alive. I catch glimpses of her in Jacob's broken heart, in dark-eyed Joseph and squalling little Benjamin. Seven children God has given me with Jacob! And still he loves Rachel more. Should my husband and I live another hundred years, I will never be his only wife. Yet who even notices my tears? Should they flood the desert, no one would care."

Contrary to what Leah may have felt, God had taken note of her sorrow. Knowing well that Jacob's heart was too cramped a space to shelter both Rachel and Leah, he made Leah a mother seven times. With each child the unhappy Leah hoped to secure her husband's affection. But each time her disappointment grew.

Still, she thanked God for her children. And she thanked him for his protection as they returned to the land he had promised Abraham and his heirs. Along the way, God had blessed Jacob's meeting with his estranged brother Esau. But Leah's joy at the brothers' friendly reunion was eclipsed by her sorrow at once again being proved the lesser-loved wife.

For Jacob had placed Rachel and her children last in their long caravan, giving them the best chance of escape should Esau and his men turn violent.

But Jacob's love could not prevent Rachel from dying in childbirth. Leah, not Rachel, was destined to be his first and last wife. Alongside her husband, the father of Israel, she would be revered as a mother of Israel. In fact, Jesus, the long-awaited Messiah, would come not through Rachel's children but through Leah's. And, in the end, Jacob was laid to rest next to his first wife, Leah, rather than his favorite wife, Rachel.

The two sisters remind us that life is fraught with sorrow and peril, much of it caused by our selfishness. Both women suffered—each in her own way. While Rachel died giving birth to a child, Leah experienced the anguish of loving a man who seemed indifferent to her. Yet both women played essential roles in the story of God's plan for his people.

Your hands shaped me and made me,
  O God.

JOB 10:8

The Spirit of God has made me;
the breath of the Almighty
  gives me life.

JOB 33:4

You created my inmost being, O
  LORD;
  you knit me together
  in my mother's womb.
I praise you because I am fearfully
and wonderfully made;
  your works are wonderful,
  I know that full well.

PSALM 139:13–14

~For Prayer~

Just like Leah, many women today suffer the painful experience of their husband's indifference, making them question their own worth. If you are one of those women, or even if you're not, take time today to thank God for making you the woman you are. Remember that he loves you and has made you in his image. Call to mind what you like about yourself—your quirky sense of humor, your love of great literature, your compassion for other people, your curly hair, even the shape of your toes. And resist the temptation to think about what you don't like.

Lord, I don't want to be critical of how you've put me together, relying on what others think of me for my sense of well-being. Make me a woman who is confident she is lovable, not because of any outward beauty but because you have loved me from the moment you made me.

Potiphar's Wife

Potiphar's Wife

Potiphar's Wife

Her name is

unknown, but

the story of her

unrequited passion

is memorable.

Joseph lived in the house of his Egyptian master. ... Potiphar put him in charge of his household. ... Now Joseph was well-built and handsome, and after a while his master's wife took notice of Joseph and said, "Come to bed with me!"

But he refused. ...

One day he went into the house to attend to his duties, and none of the household servants was inside. She caught him by his cloak and said, "Come to bed with me!" But he left his cloak in her hand and ran out of the house. ...

She kept his cloak beside her until his master came home. Then she told him this story: "That Hebrew slave you brought us came to me to make sport of me. But as soon as I screamed for help, he left his cloak beside me and ran out of the house."

When his master heard the story his wife told him ... [he] took Joseph and put him in prison.

GENESIS 39:2, 4, 6–8, 11–12, 16–20

Her Character

The wife of a prosperous and influential Egyptian, she was unfaithful and vindictive, ready to lie in order to protect herself and ruin an innocent man.

Her Sorrow

To be rebuffed by a slave.

We don't even know her name. She is merely presented as the spoiled wife of a prosperous Egyptian official, determined to seduce the handsome young Hebrew slave, Joseph.

The favorite child of Rachel and Jacob, Joseph seems to have unwittingly done everything possible to ensure his brothers' enmity, even recounting a dream predicting that he, the younger son, would one day rule over them. Envious, the brothers faked his death and sold him to slave traders enroute to Egypt.

There Potiphar, the captain of the guard, bought the young man and gradually entrusted him with responsibility for his entire household. Joseph so impressed Potiphar's wife that she made her admiration obvious by inviting him to share her bed. Joseph, however, politely refused.

Though it must have galled her to be rebuffed by a slave, she was undeterred. Her opportunity came one day when she and Joseph were alone in the house. Catching his cloak, she whispered, "Lie with me!"

But Joseph fled, leaving his would-be seducer alone with her lust, furiously clutching his cloak in her fingers.

Fearing perhaps that Joseph would speak to Potiphar about what had happened, she wasted no time accusing him of attempted rape. When her husband heard the news, he was outraged, quickly consigning his favorite servant to prison.

The story of Joseph and how God blessed him even in his prison cell, eventually enabling him to become master of the nation he had entered as a slave, is well known to us. But we haven't a clue about Potiphar's wife. Whatever became of her? Did her husband suspect her duplicity? Is that why he merely confined Joseph to prison rather than executing him, as he had every right to do? Potiphar's wife seems to have been a hollow woman, whose soul was steadily decaying through the corrosive power of lust. Surrounded by luxury, she was yet spiritually impoverished. Empty of God, she was full of herself.

*Create in me a pure heart, O God,
and renew a steadfast spirit within me.*

PSALM 51:10

*If we walk in the light, as God is in
the light, we have fellowship with one
another, and the blood of Jesus, his Son,
purifies us from all sin.*

1 JOHN 1:7

*Let us draw near to God with a sin-
cere heart in full assurance of faith, having our hearts sprinkled to cleanse us
from a guilty conscience and having our
bodies washed with pure water.*

HEBREWS 10:22

~ *For Prayer* ~

Scripture does not record what happened to Potiphar's wife after this incident with Joseph. Try writing a short account from your own imagination, entitled "Whatever Became of Potiphar's Wife." Try putting yourself in the story. You could be Potiphar's wife, her mother, her maid, her best friend—whoever you want to be. Does anything hit you as you ponder her story's conclusion?

Lord, I don't want my soul to feed on empty pleasures, to long for what belongs to someone else. Instead, increase my hunger for you and create in me a pure heart, one that you will find irresistibly beautiful.

Miriam

Which may mean

"bitterness."

The Israelites walked through the sea on dry ground. Then Miriam the prophetess, Aaron's sister, took a tambourine in her hand, and all the women followed her, with tambourines and dancing. ...

EXODUS 15:19–20

Miriam and Aaron began to talk against Moses. ...

At once the Lord said to Moses, Aaron and Miriam, "Come out to the Tent of Meeting, all three of you." ... Then the Lord ... summoned Aaron and Miriam. . . .

The anger of the Lord burned against them, and he left them.

When the cloud lifted from above the Tent, there stood Miriam—leprous, like snow. ...

So Miriam was confined outside the camp for seven days, and the people did not move on till she was brought back.

NUMBERS 12:1, 4–5, 9–10, 15

Her Character

A leader of God's people at a crucial moment in history, she led the celebration after crossing the Red Sea and spoke God's word to his people, sharing their forty-year journey through the wilderness.

Her Sorrow

That God afflicted her with leprosy because she opposed her brother Moses. She died before entering the Promised Land.

Her Joy

To have played an instrumental role in the deliverance of God's people.

"Seven days I must stay outside the camp of my people, an old woman, fenced in by memories of what has been.

"How could I forget our years in Egypt, the cries of the mothers whose children were murdered or the moans of our brothers as they worked themselves to death? I have only to shut my eyes and see—the wall of water, the drowning soldiers. We sang and danced that day at the edge of the sea, praising God, certain our enemies had finally been destroyed.

"How I wish we had been right. But enemies remained. Ingratitude chased us. Fear stalked us. We were not yet free.

"Time and again Moses and Aaron and I encouraged the people to obey God, to believe the promise. But there came a day when Aaron and I spoke against Moses. 'Has the Lord spoken only through Moses,' we asked. 'Hasn't he also spoken through us?' But God became angry and afflicted me with leprosy. Moses prayed for healing, and the Lord told him I should be banished for seven days.

"Now I see that my enemies were not merely buried in the sea nor in the hearts of an obstinate people, but in my own heart as well. Still, God has let me live, and I believe he will heal me. Though he brings grief, he will yet show compassion."

Though Scripture doesn't reveal Miriam's thoughts after she was chastened for standing against Moses, it is not unreasonable to think she repented during her banishment. Perhaps Miriam, and the nation itself, needed a shocking rebuke in order to recognize the seriousness of a sin that threatened the unity of God's people. The last we hear of Miriam is that she died and was buried shortly before the Israelites entered the Promised Land. Despite her rebellion, she is one of the great heroes of our faith. As a young girl, she helped save the infant Moses, Israel's future deliverer. Herself a prophetess, she exhorted and encouraged God's people and led the singing of the first psalm ever recorded in Scripture. Strong though she was, she sinned against God and suffered a punishment designed to bring her to repentance.

*Blessed is the man whom God corrects;
so do not despise the discipline
of the Almighty.*

JOB 5:17

The LORD disciplines those he loves.

PROVERBS 3:12

*No discipline seems pleasant at the
time, but painful. Later on, however, it
produces a harvest of righteousness and
peace for those who have been trained
by it.*

HEBREWS 12:11

~For Prayer~

If a woman like Miriam could act in a way so displeasing to God, certainly we, too, are capable of sinning, no matter what we have done for him in the past. Take time this week to do a little honest soul-searching. If you discover anything displeasing to God, ask for forgiveness. Don't just whisper a quick prayer and be done with it. Instead, express your sincere repentance and thank him for his forgiveness.

***

Father, thank you for the times you've brought me up short and loved me enough to discipline me. Help me be quick to repent. Then let me experience the joy that comes from receiving your forgiveness.

***

Deborah

Which means

"honey bee."

Deborah, a prophetess, the wife of Lappidoth, was leading Israel at that time. ... She sent for Barak ... and said to him, "The LORD, the God of Israel, commands you: 'Go, take with you ten thousand men. ... I will lure Sisera ... and give him into your hands.'"

Barak said to her, "If you go with me, I will go; but if you don't go with me, I won't go."

"Very well," Deborah said, "I will go with you. But because of the way you are going about this, the honor will not be yours, for the LORD will hand Sisera over to a woman." So Deborah went with Barak. ...

At Barak's advance, ... all the troops of Sisera fell by the sword; not a man was left.

JUDGES 4:4, 6–9, 15–16

Her Character

Though women in the ancient world did not usually become political leaders, Deborah was exactly the leader Israel needed. A prophetess who heard God and believed him, her courage roused the people.

—◆—

Her Sorrow

That her people had sunk into despair because of their idolatry.

—◆—

Her Joy

That God turned the enemy's strength on its head, bestowing power to the weak and blessing the land with peace for forty years.

*J*ericho had lain in ruins for two hundred years, destroyed when the Israelites first swept into Canaan after their forty-year sojourn in the desert. But the native peoples had managed to survive and their idolatrous practices had spread until they threatened to strangle Israel's faith.

Now the Israelites were once again the underdogs, oppressed by a coalition of Canaanite rulers, whose chief warrior was Sisera. His nine hundred chariots terrified the ill-armed people.

Sisera must have felt smugly secure, especially since Israel was now led by a woman. But his military calculations failed to account for one key variable—the strategic power of that woman's faith.

Deborah was a prophetess who held court under a palm tree near Jericho. Though much of Israel was divided and dispirited, she refused to lose heart. She summoned Barak, a Jew from the north, and told him plainly: "This is what the Lord commands. Go, march on Mount Tabor, and take with you ten thousand men. I will lead Sisera and his chariots and troops out to you at the Kishon

River and will deliver them into your hands."

But, like every other man in Israel, Barak was terrified of Sisera, and he refused to comply unless one condition was met: Deborah must accompany him. She would be his talisman on the day of battle. "Very well," she replied, "I will go with you. But because of the way you are going about this, the Lord will hand Sisera over to a woman."

Hearing of the plot, Sisera led his troops and chariots to the Kishon River, determined to crush the uprising. But his strength turned against him as rain swelled the river to floodtide. Suddenly nine hundred chariots became a huge liability. No matter how furiously the soldiers flogged their horses, the oozing mud held them, making them easy targets for Barak's troops.

Once again, God had heard his people's cries and sent a deliverer—this time a woman whose strong faith gave birth to a peace that lasted forty years. Deborah led the Israelites out of idolatry and restored their dignity as God's chosen people.

The LORD himself goes before you
and will be with you; he will never leave
you nor forsake you. Do not be afraid;
do not be discouraged.

DEUTERONOMY 31:8

Come, let us bow down in worship,
let us kneel before the LORD our
Maker;
for he is our God
and we are the people of his pasture,
the flock under his care.
Today, if you hear his voice,
do not harden your hearts.

PSALM 95:6–8

~For Prayer~

It's hard to hear God's voice when you are listening to voices of confusion, discouragement, and condemnation. Deborah's peace and confidence as a leader stemmed in part from her ability to hear God clearly. This week ask the Holy Spirit to help you distinguish God's voice from all the background noise. Ask for grace to discipline your thoughts in order to hear God better.

Lord, I want to hear your voice. Help me to recognize and resist all the phony voices that masquerade as yours. Make me a woman who both listens and speaks your word.

Hannah

Which means

"graciousness" or

"favor."

Elkanah ... had two wives; one was called Hannah and the other Peninnah. Peninnah had children, but Hannah had none. ...

And because the Lord had closed her womb, her rival kept provoking her in order to irritate her ... till she wept and would not eat. ...

In bitterness of soul Hannah wept much and prayed to the LORD. And she made a vow, saying, "O LORD Almighty, if you will only look upon your servant's misery and remember me, and not forget your servant but give her a son, then I will give him to the LORD for all the days of his life." ...

Elkanah lay with Hannah his wife, and the LORD remembered her. So in the course of time Hannah conceived and gave birth to a son. She named him Samuel, saying, "Because I asked the LORD for him."

1 SAMUEL 1:1–2, 6–7, 10–11, 19–20

Her Character

Provoked by another woman's malice, she refused to respond in kind. Instead she poured out her hurt and sorrow to God.

Her Sorrow

To be taunted and misunderstood.

Her Joy

To proclaim God's power and goodness, his habit of raising the lowly and humbling the proud.

*I*t was only fifteen miles, but every year the journey to worship at the tabernacle in Shiloh seemed longer. At home Hannah found ways to avoid her husband's second wife, but once in Shiloh there was no escaping her taunts.

Even Elkanah's arms around her provided little shelter. "Hannah, why do you weep and refuse to eat? Am I not more to you than ten sons? Yes, she has given me children, but I love you. Ignore her."

How could Hannah make him understand—that even the best of men could not erase a woman's longing for children? She stood for a long time at the tabernacle. As she prayed, her shoulders shook and her lips moved silently, imploring God for a son she could dedicate to his service.

The priest Eli was used to those who came to celebrate the feasts, eating and drinking more than they should. Watching her, he thought Hannah must be drunk. So he interrupted her silent prayer with a rebuke: "How long will you make a drunken show of yourself? Sober up from your wine!"

Hannah defended herself. "I am an unhappy woman. I have had neither wine nor liquor; I was only pouring out my troubles to the Lord."

So Eli blessed her and sent her on her way.

When Hannah and Elkanah returned to their home in Ramah, Hannah conceived. Soon she held a tiny son against her breast—Samuel, the child she had dedicated to God. After he was weaned, she would take him to Eli at Shiloh and surrender her child to the priest's care. Eventually Hannah's boy would become Israel's last judge as well as a prophet and priest. His hands would anoint both Saul and David as Israel's first kings.

Like Sarah and Rachel, Hannah grieved over the children she couldn't have. Misunderstood by both her husband and her priest, she could easily have turned her sorrow on herself or others, becoming angry and vindictive. Instead, she poured out her troubles to God. And God graciously heard her.

Answer me when I call to you,
O my righteous God.
  Give me relief from my distress;
be merciful to me and hear my prayer.

PSALM 4:1

Why are you downcast, O my soul?
    Why so disturbed within me?
Put your hope in God,
    for I will yet praise him,
    my Savior and my God.
My soul is downcast within me;
    therefore I will remember you. . . .

PSALM 42:5–6

One way to build your confidence in God's willingness to hear and answer your prayers is to form a habit of remembrance. Recalling and thanking God for what he's done, builds a habit of gratitude. Find a blank notebook that can become your Remembrance Book. Write down all the ways God has answered your prayers. Recall how his answer sometimes took you by surprise—it was so ingenious, so creative. Let your Remembrance Book be a tangible way to keep God's faithfulness in the forefront of your heart.

Father, thank you for all the prayers you've answered during my lifetime—small prayers and big prayers, evening prayers and morning prayers, soft prayers and loud prayers, anxious prayers and peaceful prayers. May my own prayers be shaped according to your faithfulness, becoming less selfish and frantic and more calm and trusting with each day that passes.

Michal

Which means

"Who is like

God?"

Saul's daughter Michal was in love with David. ... "I will give her to him," he thought, "so that she may be a snare to him." ...

When Saul realized that the LORD was with David and that his daughter Michal loved David, Saul became still more afraid of him, and he remained his enemy the rest of his days.

1 SAMUEL 18:20–21, 28–29

Saul had given his daughter Michal, David's wife, to Paltiel. ...

Then David sent messengers to Ish-Bosheth son of Saul, demanding, "Give me my wife Michal." ...

So Ish-Bosheth gave orders and had her taken away from her husband Paltiel. ...

1 SAMUEL 25:44; 2 SAMUEL 3:14–15

And when [Michal] saw King David leaping and dancing before the LORD, she despised him in her heart.

2 SAMUEL 6:16

Her Character

A woman of strong emotions, she was unable to control pivotal circumstances of her life. Forcibly separated from two husbands, she lost her father and her brother in war.

Her Sorrow

That she was ensnared in the drawn-out battle between Saul and David.

Her Joy

Though short-lived, she enjoyed a passionate love for David.

Scene One

Michal leaned out of the window as far as she dared, watching David run through the night shadows. She was glad for his escape, knowing Saul meant to destroy him. Even if her father pursued with an army, she was confident he would not catch her husband.

Scene Two

Years later, Michal glanced out another window, arms folded tightly against her breast. She watched King David leaping and dancing before the ark of the covenant. He looked, she thought, more like a romping goat than a great king.

Twice, Michal stood at a window observing David. Her attitude is so changed that we feel perplexed, watching her as she watches David. Somehow, we need to find the corridor connecting the two windows, the passageway that led from love to scorn.

Perhaps Michal's idealism forged a happy ending to their fairy tale love. Was she shocked when real life intervened and her father married her to another man after David's escape?

Did her bitterness grow during David's long absence? Had she finally made peace with her new husband only to be torn from him when David demanded her back after Saul's death?

Perhaps Michal realized she was a pawn, a mere woman manipulated by powerful men. First her own father used her, marrying her to David then to another. Finally, her brother handed her back to David after Saul's death, further legitimizing David's claim to the throne. A princess, then a queen, she was yet a slave.

Michal's story is tragic. Throughout the difficult events of her life, we see little evidence of a faith to sustain her. Instead, she is tossed back and forth by circumstances, her heart left to draw its own bitter conclusions.

*David, wearing a linen ephod, danced before the L*ORD *with all his might. . . .*

2 SAMUEL 6:14

*Ascribe to the L*ORD *the glory due his name;*
    *worship the L*ORD *in the splendor of his holiness.*

PSALM 29:2

Let them praise God's name with dancing
    and make music to him with tambourine and harp.

PSALM 149:3

~For Prayer~

David's worship was so exuberant that he danced in public. You may not be quite ready to take your joy to the streets, but you can loosen up a bit by raising your hands in prayer, visiting a church whose worship style is a little outside your comfort zone, or just dancing and singing along with a praise and worship tape when no one else is home. Enjoy yourself in God's presence! If he's not worth getting excited about, who is?

Shout with joy to God, all the earth! Sing the glory of his name; make his praise glorious! Say to God, "How awesome are your deeds! ... All the earth bows down to you; they sing praise to you, they sing praise to your name" (Psalm 66:1–4).

Which means

"my father is joy."

A certain man ... was very wealthy. ... His name was Nabal and his wife's name was Abigail. She was an intelligent and beautiful woman, but [Nabal] was surly and mean in his dealings. ...

One of the servants told Nabal's wife Abigail: "David sent messengers from the desert to give our master his greetings, but he hurled insults at them. ... disaster is hanging over our ... whole household."

Abigail lost no time. ...

As she came riding her donkey into a mountain ravine, there were David and his men. ...

When Abigail saw David, she quickly ... fell at his feet and said: "My lord ... pay no attention to that wicked man Nabal. He is just like his name—his name is Fool. ...

David said to Abigail, "Praise be to the Lord, the God of Israel, who has sent you today to meet me. May you be blessed for your good judgment and for keeping me from ... avenging myself with my own hands."

About ten days later, the Lord struck Nabal and he died.

When David heard that Nabal was dead, he ... sent word to Abigail, asking her to become his wife.

1 SAMUEL 25:2–3, 14, 17–18, 20, 23–25, 32–33, 38–39

Her Character

Generous, quick-witted, and wise, she is one of the Bible's great peace-makers.

<center>~~~</center>

Her Sorrow

To have been mismatched in marriage to her first husband.

<center>~~~</center>

Her Joy

That God used her to save lives, eventually making her the wife of David.

Abigail had heard nothing but good of David, the young warrior who had taken refuge from King Saul near her home in the desert of Maon, west of the Dead Sea. David and his men had kept marauders clear of her husband Nabal's livestock. But when David sent ten men to ask for provisions, Nabal, who had grown richer thanks to David, foolishly insulted the region's most powerful man.

Learning what happened, Abigail loaded a caravan of donkeys with gifts for David and his men. She met them when they were on their way to take revenge, falling on the ground at David's feet.

"My lord, let the blame be mine. Don't pay attention to that worthless man Nabal. Fool is his name, and he acts the fool. It is the Lord who has kept you from shedding blood and from avenging yourself."

David listened closely to Abigail and then replied graciously: "Blessed be your good judgment and blessed be you yourself, who this day you have prevented me from shedding blood."

After her encounter with David, Abigail went back to Nabal. Again, she found him playing the fool, drunkenly presiding over a festival banquet. She waited until morning, when he was sober, to tell him what had happened. As soon as Nabal heard the news, his heart failed. Ten days later he was dead.

Arrogance, greed, and selfishness had robbed Nabal of any good sense he might once have possessed. Thinking himself a great man when he was only a small one, he lost everything.

Abigail was his opposite, a woman whose humility, faith, generosity, and intelligence made her wise. Her virtues were developed right in the midst of a difficult marriage. Through her quick-witted action, she spared her community. Rather than putting others at risk by an ungoverned tongue, Abigail's gracious words saved lives. And in the end, it was God, not Abigail or David, who paid Nabal back for his arrogance and greed.

When David heard the news of Nabal's death, he sent word to Abigail, asking her to be his wife. Abigail accepted, becoming David's third wife and eventually mother to his second son, Kileab.

*A wife of noble character is her hus-
band's crown. . . .*

PROVERBS 12:4

*Since the day we heard about you,
we have not stopped praying for you and
asking God to fill you with the knowledge of his will through all spiritual wisdom and understanding. And we pray
this in order that you may live a life
worthy of the Lord and may please him
in every way.*

COLOSSIANS 1:9–10

~For Prayer~

If you haven't yet made a commitment to pray daily for your husband, do so today. Set aside a few minutes to surrender your marriage to God, specifically asking him to bless your spouse. Try to refrain from focusing on your laundry list of complaints and instead pray for the needs you know he has. Ask God to shape your relationship and use it for his purposes. Relinquish any desire you may have to control your husband and instead ask God to work in his life.

Father, I ask you to bless my husband in every facet of his life—
his health
his work
his relationship with our children
our relationship together
and his relationship with you.
Let nothing and no one, including myself, hinder your work in his life.

Jehosheba

Jehosheba

Jehosheba

Jehosheba

Which means

"swear by his

name."

When Athaliah the mother of Ahaziah saw that her son was dead, she proceeded to destroy the whole royal family. But Jehosheba, the daughter of King Jehoram and sister of Ahaziah, took Joash son of Ahaziah and stole him away from among the royal princes, who were about to be murdered. She put him and his nurse in a bedroom to hide him from Athaliah; so he was not killed. He remained hidden in the temple of the Lord for six years while Athaliah ruled the land.

2 KINGS 11:1–3

Her Character

She was a courageous woman whose actions preserved the line of Judah's kings, from which the Messiah would come.

Her Joy

That she was able to preserve the life of her brother's youngest son, Joash, so that he could become rightful king of Judah.

Her Sorrow

That she endured Athaliah's reign and lost many of her nephews at the queen's hand.

Wicked queens are the stuff of fairy tales. Remember the snow queen in the tales of Hans Christian Andersen, or the evil queen in *The Lion, the Witch and the Wardrobe*? Queen Athaliah was at least as bad as her fairy-tale counterparts, a woman who chilled the hearts of God's people by killing her own grandsons in order to secure Judah's throne.

During her six-year reign, she promoted Baal worship, leading the people further away from the one true God.

But right under her nose a conspiracy was taking shape. Though she didn't know it, little Joash, one of her grandsons, was still alive, hidden in the temple by Jehosheba, Athaliah's step-daughter and wife of the high priest. For six years the younger woman risked her life to preserve her nephew's. Finally, when the boy turned seven, Jehosheba's husband arranged a coup, crowning Joash king.

As soon as Athaliah caught wind of the plot, she rushed to the temple, tearing her robes and screaming, "Treason!

Treason!" But no one paid her the slightest attention. The wicked queen had suddenly been deposed.

Jehosheba's courage and compassion helped to subvert the plans of a powerful queen. Through her courageous actions, God was answering the prayers of his people, keeping the promise of the Messiah alive.

You know with all your heart and soul that not one of all the good promises the LORD your God gave you has failed. Every promise has been fulfilled; not one has failed.

JOSHUA 23:14

Many are the plans in a man's heart, but it is the LORD's purpose that prevails.

PROVERBS 19:21

~ For Prayer ~

Imagine what Jehosheba must have felt like, not just for a moment, but for several years as she defied an evil and powerful queen. Where did she find the strength? What were her fears? Envision what her life must have been like and ask God to speak to you through her story. Let another woman's story encourage you to do what is right regardless of the risks involved.

Lord, when I am faced with evil, whether it is in government, in the church, or in my neighborhood or family, help me to do whatever is in my power to resist. Give me wisdom to know what to do, courage to act well, and grace to trust you for the outcome.

Bathsheba

Which means "the seventh daugh-ter" or "daughter of an oath."

One evening David got up from his bed and walked around on the roof of the palace. From the roof he saw a woman bathing. The woman was very beautiful. ... Then David sent messengers to get her. She came to him, and he slept with her. ... The woman conceived and sent word to David, saying, "I am pregnant." ...

David wrote a letter to Joab ... "Put Uriah in the front line where the fighting is fiercest. Then withdraw from him so he will be struck down and die." ...

When Uriah's wife heard that her husband was dead, she mourned for him. After the time of mourning was over, David had her brought to his house, and she became his wife and bore him a son. But the thing David had done displeased the LORD.

2 SAMUEL 11:2, 4–5, 14–15, 26–27

Her Character

Her beauty made her victim to a king's desire. Though it is difficult to discern her true character, she seems to have found the courage to endure tragedy, winning the king's confidence and eventually securing the kingdom for her son, Solomon.

———

Her Sorrow

To have been molested by a supposedly godly man who then murdered her husband. To have suffered the loss of her son.

———

Her Joy

To have given birth to five sons, one of whom became king of Israel after David's death.

*N*ormally, Bathsheba looked forward to the ritual bath at the end of the month. Tonight, however, the water soothed her skin without refreshing her spirit. She should be glad for the cool breeze. But spring, the season for armies and battles, inevitably brought its crop of sorrows. Though her husband Uriah was a seasoned soldier, she still worried, wishing she could fall asleep in his arms. But he was camped miles away with the king's army.

David, unable to sleep, paced the palace roof. In the half-light he noticed the figure of a young woman bathing in the garden of a house below him. Unaware of his gaze, she toweled herself dry and then stepped into the house.

The king soon discovered the vision had a name: Bathsheba, the wife of one of his soldiers, Uriah. So he sent for her, and she became pregnant with his child.

Fearing discovery, the king ordered Uriah home from battle. But, out of loyalty to the army, Uriah refused to spend the night with his wife. Even David's efforts to get him drunk did not weaken Uriah's resolve.

So the king arranged for Bathsheba's husband to be placed at the front of the battle, where he died.

Then David claimed Bathsheba as his wife.

David's lust for Bathsheba marked the beginning of his long decline. Though God forgave him, he still suffered the consequences of his wrongdoing. Despite David's pleading, God allowed Bathsheba's son to die.

But why did Bathsheba have to suffer along with the man who molested her and murdered her husband? Though we have little insight into her true character, it is hardly likely that Bathsheba was in a position to refuse the king, whose power was absolute. Why then have so many people painted her as a seductress? Perhaps Bathsheba's innocence is too painful to face. That a good person can suffer such tragedies, especially at the hands of a godly person, appalls us. Though Bathsheba may not have understood the reasons for her suffering, God gave her favor with King David, making her both a powerful queen and the mother of David's successor, Solomon, who became famous for his great wisdom.

I am in pain and distress;
   may your salvation, O God,
   protect me.

PSALM 69: 29

Rescue me and deliver me
   in your righteousness, O Lord;
turn your ear to me and save me.
   Be my rock of refuge,
to which I can always go.

PSALM 71:2–3

~For Prayer~

If you have suffered from the mistakes and sins of others, you know how hard it can be sometimes to forgive. But the alternative to forgiveness is bitterness. Take a moment to search your heart. Ask God to help you forgive those who've injured you. If hurt and anger seem to linger, remember that forgiveness sometimes takes time. Just keep deciding in your heart that you will forgive and God will give you peace.

Father, forgiveness is so hard sometimes. Please help me to begin by letting go of my desire for revenge. Every time I start wishing something negative on those who've hurt me, help me to pray a blessing on them instead. Only you can give me the desire to forgive. Only you can help me do the impossible.

Queen of Sheba

Queen of Sheba

Queen of Sheba

Though queen of a pagan nation, she was drawn to the wisdom of God.

When the queen of Sheba heard about the fame of Solomon and his relation to the name of the LORD, she came to test him with hard questions. Arriving at Jerusalem with a very great caravan—with camels carrying spices, large quantities of gold, and precious stones—she came to Solomon and talked with him about all that she had on her mind. Solomon answered all her questions; nothing was too hard for the king to explain to her. ...

She said to the king, "The report I heard in my own country about your achievements and your wisdom is true. But I did not believe these things until I came and saw with my own eyes. Indeed, not even half was told me; in wisdom and wealth you have far exceeded the report I heard. ... Praise be to the LORD your God, who has delighted in you and placed you on the throne of Israel.

1 KINGS 10:1–3, 6–7, 9

Her Character

Though a pagan queen, she prized wisdom above power. She seems to have been extremely bright, with a good head for business and diplomacy.

Her Joy

That her quest for wisdom was rewarded beyond her expectations.

Sheba was a fragrant land, famous for its perfumes and spices. Located on the southwestern tip of Arabia, bordering the Red Sea, it traded precious commodities like gold, frankincense and myrrh to kingdoms in Africa, India, and the Mediterranean. Little wonder that passing caravans brought news of the wide world to Sheba's queen.

Lately, she had heard marvelous stories of Solomon, Israel's king. Some said he was the wisest man alive. The queen had also heard of the fabulous temple and palace Solomon had built in Jerusalem.

Though Jerusalem lay 1500 miles to the north, the queen was determined to see for herself whether Solomon measured up to even half the tales told of him. So she assembled a caravan of camels and loaded them with precious spices, gems and a mere four-and-a-half tons of gold. Her entrance into Jerusalem created an unforgettable spectacle, adding to Solomon's growing fame.

Day after day, the queen pounded Solomon with hard questions. But nothing was too difficult for him to explain.

Finally she exclaimed: "The report I heard in my country is true. Though I did not believe it until I came and saw with my own eyes, I have discovered that they were not telling me the half. Blessed be the LORD, your God, whom it has pleased to place you on the throne of Israel." Then the queen gave Solomon all the gold and spices she had brought with her, perhaps foreshadowing the Magi's gift of gold, frankincense, and myrrh to the Christ child nearly a thousand years later.

Jesus himself referred to the Queen of Sheba when he replied to the Pharisees who demanded from him a miraculous sign: "The Queen of the South will rise at the judgment with this generation and condemn it; for she came from the ends of the earth to listen to Solomon's wisdom, and now one greater than Solomon is here." Though queen of a pagan nation, she was drawn to the wisdom of God. She made an arduous and dangerous journey in order to meet the world's wisest man. Surely, she must have thought the price worth paying.

The fear of the LORD is the beginning of wisdom;
*   all who follow his precepts have good understanding.*
*   To him belongs eternal praise.*

PSALM 111:10

Knowledge of the Holy One is understanding.

PROVERBS 9:10

Wisdom has nothing to do with how many "gray cells" you possess. You can be smart as a whip but still full of foolishness. Take a few moments to reflect on this condensed and paraphrased passage from Proverbs 3:13–18: "Happy is the woman who finds wisdom. She has found something more precious than gold. None of her possessions can compare with wisdom. For wisdom brings long life, riches, honor, and peace. Wisdom is a tree of life to be embraced."

Lord, you are the source of the wisdom that brings life, wealth, honor, and peace. May wisdom be like a growing tree in my life, bearing abundant fruit for your kingdom.

Huldah

Which means

"weasel."

When [Josiah] heard the words of the Law, he tore his robes. He gave these orders: ... "Go and inquire of the LORD ... about what is written in this book that has been found. Great is the LORD's anger that is poured out on us because our fathers have not kept the word of the LORD." ...

[Those] the king had sent ... went to speak to the prophetess Huldah. ...

She said to them, "This is what the LORD, the God of Israel, says: Tell the man who sent you to me, 'This is what the LORD says: I am going to bring disaster on this place and its people ... because they have forsaken me and burned incense to other gods. ... Tell the king of Judah ... because your heart was responsive and you humbled yourself before God. ... I will gather you to your fathers, and you will be buried in peace.'"

2 Chronicles 34:19–28

Her Character

Trusted by the king with a matter of great importance, she was a prophetess whose word generated a significant religious reform.

Her Sorrow

That God's people refused to respond to him with loving obedience, ignoring repeated warnings about the consequences of their unfaithfulness.

Her Joy

As a prophetess, she was privileged to be a messenger of God.

*H*uldah pressed the scroll against her breast, as though cradling a living being. The high priest stood before her. King Josiah wanted to know—would the words of the Book of the Law, which had been discovered in the temple, come to pass?

Carefully she unrolled the scroll and began reading: "You shall love the Lord your God, with all your heart and soul and strength. Do not follow other gods, for the Lord your God, who is among you, is a jealous God and his anger will burn against you, and he will destroy you from the face of the land."

Visions from the past rose in her mind: kings sacrificing their sons to pagan deities … the smoke of incense rising before pagan idols in God's temple … prophets being murdered.

Still holding the scroll, she spoke these words: "The Lord says: I am prepared to bring evil on this place because these people have abandoned me and offered incense to other gods. My anger is ablaze against this place and cannot be extinguished."

Beyond this brief scene, we know little of Huldah's story—only that God entrusted her with his word in a time of national crisis. A hundred years earlier, God had punished the Northern Kingdom, allowing faithless Israel to be led captive to Assyria, just as the prophets had warned. Huldah surely knew the sordid details. She could not have missed its frightening significance for the Southern Kingdom of Judah.

Her words of prophecy confirmed the king's fear. Judah was standing at the brink of a terrible judgment. God's slow anger was building to a fiery crescendo. Thirty-five years after Huldah's prophecy, despite a time of religious reform under Josiah, Judah was taken in chains to Babylon and all of its cities were destroyed.

The magnificent kingdom of David and Solomon had finally come to its end. But though every other nation captured by Assyria and Babylon ceased to exist, Israel still had a future. Chastened, it was never destroyed. Disciplined, it was never forsaken. ... Huldah was a woman who understood the paradox and who was not afraid to proclaim the truth—even to a king. She cherished God's word in a time of spiritual crisis.

Then I acknowledged my sin to you
    and did not cover up my iniquity.
I said, "I will confess
    my transgressions to the LORD"—
and you forgave
    the guilt of my sin.

PSALM 32:5

At one time we too were foolish. ...
But when the kindness and love of God
our Savior appeared, he saved us, not
because of righteous things we had done,
but because of his mercy. He saved us
through the washing of rebirth and
renewal by the Holy Spirit, whom he
poured out on us generously through
Jesus Christ our Savior. . . .

TITUS 3:3–6

~For Prayer~

Our hearts can become hardened by disobedience in both small and large matters. Set aside a day to conduct a little spring cleaning of your soul. Ask yourself the tough questions. Is there anything you cherish—money, power, a person—more than God? Have you ever hurt someone with hateful words? Have you ever stolen someone's reputation through envy? Have you ever rejoiced at someone else's misfortune? Don't wallow in your failings. Admit them and then ask for God's forgiveness and the grace to change.

Father, may I have ears to hear your word and a heart to obey it. Cleanse me from my sin and wash me until I am whiter than snow. Make my soul clean and pure, a broad and spacious place for your Spirit to dwell.

Esther

Which may come

from "Ishtar," the

Babylonian goddess

of love or from the

Persian word for

"star."

Mordecai had a cousin named [Esther], whom he had brought up because she had neither father nor mother. This girl ... was lovely in form and features. ...

Now the king was attracted to Esther more than to any of the other women. ... So he set a royal crown on her head and made her queen. ...

Mordecai told [Hathach] everything that had happened to him, including the exact amount of money Haman had promised to pay into the royal treasury for the destruction of the Jews. He ... told [Hathach] to urge [Esther] to go into the king's presence to beg for mercy and plead with him for her people.

Then Esther sent this reply to Mordecai: "Go, gather together all the Jews who are in Susa, and fast for me. Do not eat or drink for three days, night or day. I and my maids will fast as you do. When this is done, I will go to the king, even though it is against the law. And if I perish, I perish."

ESTHER 2:7, 17; 4:7–8, 15–16

Her Character

An orphan in a foreign land, she displayed great courage in the midst of a crisis. Prior to risking her life for her people, she humbled herself by fasting, and then put her considerable beauty, social grace, and wisdom in the service of God's plan.

Her Sorrow

To learn that her husband, the king, had unwittingly placed her life and the life of her people in jeopardy.

Her Joy

To watch mourning turn to celebration once the Jews enjoyed relief from their enemies.

*Q*ueen Vashti had so offended her husband, Xerxes, that a search was conducted for a queen to replace her. Many Jews, including Mordecai and his orphaned cousin Esther, were living in Persia at the time. Like other beautiful young women, Esther was gathered into the king's harem. Before long, she became queen in Vashti's place.

Sometime later, a man named Haman, who hated the Jews, rose to power. Devising a plot to destroy them, he consulted his gods by casting lots (or *pur*) in order to ascertain the best time to carry out his scheme. A date eleven months into the future was revealed. Unaware that Queen Esther was a Jew, he immediately persuaded Xerxes to issue a decree allowing Jews to be slaughtered on that day.

Mordecai immediately contacted Esther, asking her to intervene with Xerxes. But to come into the king's presence without an invitation was a capital offense. So Esther instructed Mordecai to mobilize all the Jews of the city to fast. She did the same, resolving, "I will go to the king. If I perish, I perish!"

When Esther approached the king, Xerxes welcomed her, promising her up to half his kingdom.

But Esther merely invited the king and Haman to join her for a feast. At the feast, the king implored Esther to ask for whatever her heart desired. This time she spoke without hesitation: "I ask, O king, that my life be spared, and I beg that you spare the lives of my people. For my people and I have been delivered to slaughter and extinction."

"Who is the man who has dared to do this?" the king demanded.

"The enemy oppressing us is this wicked Haman."

And so Haman's star, which had risen to so great a height, fell suddenly. He was hanged, and all his property was given to Esther. The king issued an edict giving Jews throughout the empire the right to protect themselves. The very day Haman's gods had revealed as a day of reckoning for the Jews became a day of reckoning for their enemies. Ever after, the Jews commemorated these events with the feast of Purim, celebrating the day when God so marvelously turned the tables on their foes.

I sat down and wept. For some days I mourned and fasted and prayed before the God of heaven. Then I said: "O LORD, God of heaven, the great and awesome God, who keeps his covenant of love with those who love him and obey his commands, let your ear be attentive and your eyes open to hear the prayer your servant is praying."

NEHEMIAH 1:4–6

When you fast, put oil on your head and wash your face, so that it will not be obvious to men that you are fasting, but only to your Father, who is unseen; and your Father, who sees what is done in secret, will reward you.

MATTHEW 6:17–18

One way we can emulate Esther today is by fasting. Before Esther acted, she employed a time-honored spiritual discipline. Fasting was a visible sign of her dependency and weakness, an eloquent form of begging God's help. This week, choose a day to fast from breakfast and lunch, perhaps even dinner. Drink only water or fruit juice. Use the time you would have spent eating to be alone with God. Tell God that you need him more than you need food. Don't try to manipulate him by your self-sacrifice, but simply allow your weakness to emerge in his presence.

⚓

Lord, I need you more than I need food or water. Without your presence, your protection, your wisdom, I would be lost. I'm hungry for you alone. Hear my prayer and give me everything I need to do your will. Use me in the church and the world around me to accomplish your purposes.

⚓

The Woman of Proverbs 31

The Woman of
Proverbs 31

A woman without a name, she is in some sense every woman who seeks to live a worthy life.

A wife of noble character who can find?

> *She is worth far more than rubies.*
> *Her husband has full confidence in her*
>> *and lacks nothing of value.*
> *She brings him good, not harm,*
>> *all the days of her life. ...*
> *She is clothed with strength and dignity;*
>> *she can laugh at the days to come.*
> *She speaks with wisdom,*
>> *and faithful instruction is on her tongue. ...*
> *Her children arise and call her blessed;*
>> *her husband also, and he praises her:*
> *"Many women do noble things,*
>> *but you surpass them all."*

PROVERBS 31:10–12, 25–26, 28–29

Her Character

She represents the fulfillment of a life lived in wisdom.

—⁓—

Her Joy

To be praised by her husband and children as a woman who surpasses all others.

*P*roverbs brims with less-than-glowing descriptions of women. There are wayward wives, prostitutes, loud women, defiant women, wives who are like a continual drip on a rainy day, women whose feet never stay home, brazen-faced women, and even a woman so repulsive she is compared to a gold ring in a pig's snout!

Any woman reading Proverbs may be tempted to conclude that its male authors despised women. But to balance things out there are at least a few odious descriptions of men, including scoundrels, chattering fools, and sluggards. And Proverbs actually opens and closes with positive portrayals of women: first as wisdom personified and then as a woman who can do no wrong.

But just who was this woman on a pedestal described in Proverbs 31? The poem describes a woman with a large household to direct. She was hard working, enterprising, wise, skilled, generous, thoughtful of others, dignified, God-fearing—a tremendous credit to her husband. Is she, as many think, a picture of the ideal wife and mother?

The description of the woman in Proverbs 31 actually offers a refreshing contrast to other ancient depictions of women, which tend to portray them in more frivolous and decorative terms. Still the perfect woman of Proverbs 31 hasn't always been a friend to ordinary women. In fact, she has sometimes been rubbed into the faces of lesser women by critical husbands and preachers. What woman could ever measure up to her? And is a woman's worth to be measured only by what she can accomplish in the domestic sphere? Or was the woman in Proverbs 31 a symbol of all the contributions a woman could make within the culture of her day? Regardless of how you answer these questions, there is more to her story than simply being the ideal wife and mother.

The woman of Proverbs 31 may well be meant to inspire both men and women with a picture of what a virtuous life is capable of producing—shelter for others, serenity, honor, prosperity, generosity, confidence about the future—true blessedness. Who wouldn't want to be like such a woman? Who wouldn't sing her praises?

The LORD gives wisdom,
*   and from his mouth come*
*   knowledge and understanding.*

PROVERBS 2:6

Wisdom is supreme; therefore get
*   wisdom.*
Though it cost all you have, get
*   understanding.*

PROVERBS 4:7

Wisdom is more precious than
rubies,
*   and nothing you desire can compare*
with her.

PROVERBS 8:11

~For Prayer~

Proverbs is full of pithy statements that contain profound wisdom for daily life. Look through this book of Scripture and select a few favorites, then commit them to memory. Here's one to get you started: "She who gets wisdom loves her own soul."

Lord, you know better than I the kind of heart in which wisdom grows best—one in which patience, faith, and humility are there to nourish it. Help me cultivate a heart in which wisdom can quickly take root and flourish. Let wisdom be so much a part of my life that it produces a shelter for others.

Mary,
Jesus
Mother

Mary Jesus
Mother

She heard the promise every Jewish woman longed to hear.

This is how the birth of Jesus Christ came about: His mother Mary was pledged to be married to Joseph, but before they came together, she was found to be with child through the Holy Spirit. Because Joseph her husband was a righteous man and did not want to expose her to public disgrace, he had in mind to divorce her quietly.

But ... an angel of the Lord appeared to him in a dream and said, "Joseph son of David, do not be afraid to take Mary home as your wife, because what is conceived in her is from the Holy Spirit. She will give birth to a son, and you are to give him the name Jesus, because he will save his people from their sins." ...

When Joseph woke up, he did what the angel of the Lord had commanded him.

MATTHEW 1:18–21, 24

Her Character

Her unqualified yes to God's plan for her life entailed great personal risk and suffering. She must have endured seasons of confusion, fear and darkness as events unfolded. She is honored, not only as the mother of Jesus, but as his first disciple.

Her Sorrow

To see the son she loved shamed and tortured, left to die like the worst kind of criminal.

Her Joy

To see her son raised from the dead; to have received the Holy Spirit along with Christ's other disciples.

*M*ary sat down on the bench and closed her eyes, an old woman silhouetted against the blue Jerusalem sky. In her mind's eye she recalled scenes from long ago ...

A cool breeze teased at her skirts as she moved across the field, balancing the empty jug on her head. Before she could dip the jug into the well, a stranger caught her attention:

"Greetings, favored one!" he shouted as he approached. "The Lord is with you."

With each step his words grew bolder, not softer, rushing toward her like water plunging over a cliff.

"Do not be afraid, Mary, for you have found favor with God. You will conceive and bear a son, and you will name him Jesus."

Wave after wave broke over her as she listened to the angel's words—first confusion and fear, then awe and gratitude, and finally a rush of joy and peace. Words of acceptance and praise cascaded from her lips: "I am the Lord's servant. May it be done to me as you have said."

Though the angel departed, Mary's peace remained. The Most High had visited the lowliest of his servants and spoken the promise every Jewish woman longed to hear.

———

"Woman," Jesus breathed the word softly. His arms were flung out on either side of him, his wrists fixed to the wood with rope, his palms pinned with spikes. She wanted to hold him in her arms again, to comfort him as though he were still a boy. Would not the God who pitied Abraham also pity her? Would he allow her to suffer what even the patriarch had been spared—the sacrifice of her own child? Isaac had escaped. Why not Jesus?

His sudden cry pierced her like a sword through the heart: "My God, my God, why have you forsaken me?" The earth shook, and she fell to her knees. ...

———

When Mary opened her eyes, the setting sun had turned the city into a golden land. So much had happened in the years since Jesus' death and resurrection. She smiled, wiping the tears from her wrinkled face. Yes, the past was alive inside her, but it was the future that filled her with joy. Soon, she would see her son again, and this time it would be his hands that would wipe away the last of her tears.

My soul glorifies the Lord
and my spirit rejoices in God my
  Savior,
for he has been mindful
  of the humble state of his servant.
From now on all generations will call
  me blessed,
for the Mighty One has done great
  things for me—
holy is his name.

LUKE 1:46–49

*Now the Lord is the Spirit, and
where the Spirit of the Lord is, there is
freedom. And we … are being transformed into his likeness with ever-
increasing glory, which comes from the
Lord, who is the Spirit.*

2 CORINTHIANS 3:17–18

~ For Prayer ~

Choose one episode in Mary's life and try to imagine yourself in her place. Ask the Holy Spirit to guide your reflections, to help you imagine the sounds, sights, and smells that will bring each scene to life. Let the Scriptures feed your soul with a deeper understanding of God's intention for your life. Pray for the grace to be like the woman who said: "I am the Lord's servant. May it be to me as you have said."

✒

My soul is full of you, my God, and I cannot hold back my gladness. You saw my lowliness and my need and filled my emptiness with your presence. Form your likeness in me so that, like Mary, I can bring you into a world that desperately needs your love.

✒

Which means

"grace."

When the time of their purification according to the Law of Moses had been completed, Joseph and Mary took [Jesus] to Jerusalem to present him to the Lord. . . .

[In Jerusalem] there was ... a prophetess, Anna. ... She was very old; she had lived with her husband seven years after her marriage, and then was a widow until she was eighty-four. She never left the temple but worshiped night and day, fasting and praying. Coming up to them at that very moment, she gave thanks to God and spoke about the child to all who were looking forward to the redemption of Jerusalem.

LUKE 2:22, 36–38

Her Character

Married for only seven years, she spent the long years of her widowhood fasting and praying in the temple, abandoning herself entirely to God. A prophetess, she was one of the first to bear witness to Jesus.

Her Sorrow

As a widow, she would probably have been among the most vulnerable members of society.

Her Joy

That her own eyes saw the Messiah.

A small bird darted past the Court of the Gentiles, flew up to the Women's Court and then on to the Court of Israel (one of the inner courts of the temple, accessible only to Jewish men). Anna blinked as she watched the beating wings swerve into the sunlight and vanish. She wondered into which privileged sanctuary the little bird had disappeared.

For most of her eighty-four years, she had been a widow who spent her days praying and fasting in the temple. She was grateful for the privilege of ascending beyond the Court of the Gentiles to the Women's Court, where she would be that much closer to the Most Holy Place. She bowed her head, rocking back and forth to the rhythm of her prayers:

"How lovely is your dwelling place
O Lord Almighty!
As the sparrow finds a home
And the swallow a nest to settle her
young,
My home is by your altars,
Lord of hosts, my king and my God!"

Suddenly a voice interrupted her recitation of the familiar psalm.

Old Simeon, she saw, was holding a baby to his chest, speaking words that thrilled her soul: "My eyes have seen your salvation."

Anna placed her arms gently around the young mother's shoulders and gazed at the sleeping infant. Words of thanksgiving spilled from her lips. A widow and prophetess from the tribe of Asher, the least in Israel, had seen the salvation of her God.

Now she, too, felt like a sparrow soaring freely in the house of God. It no longer mattered that she was forbidden entry into the innermost courts of the temple. God himself was breaking down the dividing walls between Jew and Gentile, male and female, revealing himself to all who hungered for his presence.

That day the child Jesus had transformed the Court of the Women into the holiest place of all. More vividly than Jacob, who had dreamed of a ladder full of angels, or Moses, who had beheld a bush burning in the desert, Anna had experienced the very presence of God. Her eyes had seen the promised child, whose brilliance would scatter the darkness and bring deliverance for all God's people.

Pray in the Spirit on all occasions with all kinds of prayers and requests. With this in mind, be alert and always keep on praying for all the saints.

Pray also for me, that whenever I open my mouth, words may be given me so that I will fearlessly make known the mystery of the gospel, for which I am an ambassador in chains. Pray that I may declare it fearlessly, as I should.

EPHESIANS 6:18–20

There is neither Jew nor Greek, slave nor free, male nor female, for you are all one in Christ Jesus.

GALATIANS 3:28

Pray for us that the message of the Lord may spread rapidly and be honored. . . .

2 THESSALONIANS 3:1

~For Prayer~

Anna did more than merely long for the Messiah. She prayed and fasted daily for the coming of God's kingdom. Even though Christianity has spread across the globe, there are still many people who need our dedicated prayers. Many who suffer from war and injustice, many who have little or nothing to eat, and many more who live in spiritual darkness. This week look at an atlas, a map or a globe, and choose a country for which to pray. Fast and pray for peace, for food, for freedom and justice, and for Christ's light to shine on that people.

Jesus, I long for your light to spread across the whole earth so that people from every land will know you. Today, give me a burden for another nation or ethnic group that knows little of you. Show me how to pray in a way that builds your kingdom.

The Syrophoenician Woman

The
Syrophoenician
Woman

Her name is unknown, but her persistence before Jesus is admirable.

Jesus ... went to the vicinity of Tyre. He entered a house and did not want anyone to know it; yet he could not keep his presence secret. In fact, as soon as she heard about him, a woman whose little daughter was possessed by an evil spirit came and fell at his feet. The woman was a Greek, born in Syrian Phoenicia. She begged Jesus to drive the demon out of her daughter.

"First let the children eat all they want," he told her, "for it is not right to take the children's bread and toss it to their dogs."

"Yes, Lord," she replied, "but even the dogs under the table eat the children's crumbs."

Then he told her, "For such a reply, you may go; the demon has left your daughter."

She went home and found her child lying on the bed, and the demon gone.

MARK 7:24–30

Her Character

Though a Gentile, she addressed Jesus as "Lord, Son of David." Her great faith resulted in her daughter's deliverance.

Her Sorrow

That an evil spirit possessed her child.

Her Joy

That Jesus freed her daughter.

*H*er body jerked and twisted, arms thrashing the air. Dark hair stuck in gummy strands against her cheeks. Her mother wondered what had become of her sweet child. The woman had hardly slept these last few nights for fear of what her daughter might do to herself.

That morning she heard of a Jewish healer who had come to Tyre to escape the crowds that mobbed him in Galilee. It didn't matter that Jews seldom mingled with Gentiles. She would go to him, beg his help, throw a fit herself if necessary.

As soon as she found Jesus, she pleaded, "Have pity on me, Son of David! My daughter is tormented by a demon." But he ignored her.

The woman fell at his feet again, imploring, "Lord, help me!"

Then Jesus turned and said, "It is not right to take the food of the children and throw it to the dogs."

"Please, Lord," she said, "even the dogs eat the scraps that fall from the table."

"Woman, great is your faith! It is done for you as you wish," Jesus said. And her daughter was instantly healed.

Though most of our children will never suffer from demonic possession, all of them are engaged, as we are, in a spiritual battle. As a mother, aunt, grandmother, or friend, your prayers play a role in the spiritual protection of children. Imagine that all your loved ones are surrounded by God, just as mountains surround the city of Jerusalem. Offer each one to him, placing them in his care. When you are worried about particular family members or friends, pray a quick prayer asking God to surround them with his protection.

Lord, surround my loved ones like the mountains surrounding Jerusalem. Encircle them with your power and peace. Deliver us from evil now and forever. Amen.

Mary of Bethany

Mary of
Bethany

Mary seems to have pursued one thing above all—the deepest possible relationship with Jesus.

Now a man named Lazarus was sick. He was from Bethany, the village of Mary and her sister Martha. ... So the sisters sent word to Jesus, "Lord, the one you love is sick." ...

On his arrival, Jesus found that Lazarus had already been in the tomb for four days. ...

"Take away the stone," he said. ...

So they took away the stone. Jesus called in a loud voice, "Lazarus, come out!" The dead man came out. ...

Jesus said to them, "Take off the grave clothes and let him go." ...

Six days before the Passover, Jesus arrived at Bethany. ... Here a dinner was given in Jesus' honor. Martha served, while Lazarus was among those reclining at the table with him. Then Mary took about a pint of pure nard, an expensive perfume; she poured it on Jesus' feet and wiped his feet with her hair. And the house was filled with the fragrance of the perfume.

JOHN 11:1, 3, 17, 39, 41, 43–44;
JOHN 12:1–3

Her Character

Mary appears to have been a single woman, totally devoted to Jesus. As Jesus neared the time of his triumphal entry into Jerusalem prior to Passover, she performed a gesture of great prophetic significance.

Her Sorrow

She wept at the tomb of her brother, Lazarus, and must have experienced great sorrow at the death of Jesus.

Her Joy

To have done something beautiful for Christ.

*J*erusalem was swollen with worshipers in advance of the annual Passover feast. Every one of them, it seemed, had heard tales of the rabbi Jesus and how he had raised Lazarus from the dead.

And all the while people kept chasing after Mary, inquiring about her brother. Had he really been dead four days? Didn't he smell when he came stumbling out of the tomb?

She could hardly blame them for their crazy questions. Why shouldn't they be curious? After all, it hadn't been your everyday kind of miracle. She felt a rush of joy whenever she looked at Lazarus.

But shadows framed the edges of her happiness. No amount of celebrating could erase the memory of Jesus as he wept before her brother's tomb.

Later, when Jesus arrived at Bethany just before Passover, her sister Martha served a feast in his honor. As Jesus was reclining at table with the other guests, Mary anointed his feet with a pint of expensive perfume.

The disciple, Judas Iscariot, objected: "Why was this oil not sold and the money given to the poor?"

But rather than scolding Mary, Jesus praised her: "Why do you make trouble for the woman? The poor you will always have with you; but you will not always have me. In pouring this perfume on my body, she prepared me for burial. Wherever the gospel is proclaimed, what she has done will also be told in memory of her." A short while later, he was crucified.

From her first encounter with Christ, Mary seems to have pursued one thing above all—the deepest possible relationship with him. Somehow, she must have understood that Jesus would not enter Jerusalem to lasting acclaim but to death and dishonor. While everyone else was busy celebrating his triumph, Mary stood quietly beside him, sharing his grief. She was a prophet whose gesture speaks eloquently even from a distance of 2,000 years.

How beautiful on the mountains
  are the feet of those who bring good
news,
who proclaim peace,
  who bring good tidings,
  who proclaim salvation,
who say to Zion,
  "Your God reigns!"

ISAIAH 52:7

Thanks be to God, who always leads us in triumphal procession in Christ and through us spreads everywhere the fragrance of the knowledge of him. For we are to God the aroma of Christ among those who are being saved and those who are perishing.

2 CORINTHIANS 2:14–15

~For Prayer~

How easy it is for us to neglect God by always asking him to do things for us rather than considering what we can do for him. We don't have to travel halfway around the world to do something beautiful for God. Look for a way today to bring his light to those in your own household or community who are emotionally impoverished, isolated, or ill. Even the smallest gesture performed in love can become a gift for God.

Lord, you have done so many beautiful things for me, pursuing me when I cared nothing for you, restoring my hope, giving me a future. I want to offer myself generously, not as a miser doling out her favors in hope of a return, but as a woman completely in love with her Maker. Make my life a sweet-smelling fragrance to please you.

Salome, Mother of the zebedees,

Salome, Mother of
the zebedees,

Which is a feminine

form of Solomon

and means "peace."

Then the mother of Zebedee's sons came to Jesus with her sons and, kneeling down, asked a favor of him.

"What is it you want?" he asked.

She said, "Grant that one of these two sons of mine may sit at your right and the other at your left in your kingdom."

"You don't know what you are asking," Jesus said to them. "Can you drink the cup I am going to drink?"

"We can," they answered.

Jesus said to them, "You will indeed drink from my cup, but to sit at my right or left is not for me to grant. These places belong to those for whom they have been prepared by my Father."

MATTHEW 20:20–23

Her Character

A devoted follower of Jesus, she shared the common misconception that the Messiah would drive out the Romans and establish a literal kingdom in Palestine.

Her Sorrow

To have stood with other women at the cross, witnessing the death of Jesus of Nazareth.

Her Joy

To have seen an angel at Christ's tomb, who proclaimed the resurrection.

Salome loved Jesus nearly as much as she loved her two sons, James and John. She would never forget the day they left their father and their fishing nets to follow him. She smiled when she heard Jesus had nicknamed them "the Sons of Thunder." Surely he recognized the seeds of greatness in the two feisty brothers.

Salome herself had left behind her home on the northwest shore of Galilee to join her sons. Now, as they journeyed up to Jerusalem, she remembered other words Jesus had spoken: "Ask and it will be given to you." She would no longer deny herself the one favor her heart desired. Kneeling before Jesus, she begged: "Let one of my sons sit at your right and the other at your left in your kingdom."

Instead of replying to her, Jesus turned to James and John and said, "Can you drink the cup I am going to drink?"

"We can," they answered.

Jesus said to them, "My cup you will indeed drink, but to sit at my right and left is not mine but the Father's to give."

Like any loving mother, Salome simply asked for what she thought would make her children happy. But as subsequent events proved, she didn't begin to comprehend what she was asking. Soon, the man she had approached on her knees as a king would himself die on a cross. And she would witness the gruesome spectacle. After it was over, she may have remembered the anguished faces of the men who were crucified with Jesus, one on his right, the other on his left—an ironic reminder of her request.

Salome must have forgotten that Jesus had exhorted his followers to leave behind not only houses, brothers and sisters, fathers and mothers, but also children. In Salome's case, it didn't mean turning her back on her children but surrendering them to God. It meant putting Jesus above everything and everyone, loving him better than she loved her own sons. Only then would she understand the meaning of their suffering. Only then would she really know how to pray.

Sitting down, Jesus called the Twelve and said, "If anyone wants to be first, he must be the very last, and the servant of all."

MARK 9:35

Do nothing out of selfish ambition or vain conceit, but in humility consider others better than yourselves. Each of you should look not only to your own interests, but also to the interests of others.

PHILIPPIANS 2:3–4

Who is wise and understanding among you? Let him show it by his good life, by deeds done in the humility that comes from wisdom.

JAMES 3:13

Instead of recognizing their own inherent dignity, many women have defined their worth primarily in terms of others. If you have been living your life through your husband or children, ask God for the grace to change. Admit that you need care, consideration, and replenishment. Ask God to restore balance in your life. But as you go through the process, don't eliminate the word "humility" from your vocabulary by embracing a life of selfishness. Right now, ask for eyes to see another's need and grace to serve in a way that truly models the humility of Jesus.

Lord, forgive me for any pride that has crowded you out of my heart. Whenever I am tempted to think or act with selfish ambition, place a check in my spirit. Give me, instead, the courage to be a servant.

Mary Magdalene

Magdalene origi-

nates from Mary's

hometown of

Magdala.

While it was still dark, Mary Magdalene went to the tomb and saw that the stone had been removed from the entrance. ...

Mary stood outside the tomb crying. As she wept, she bent over to look into the tomb and saw two angels. ... They asked her, "Woman, why are you crying?"

"They have taken my Lord away," she said, "and I don't know where they have put him." At this, she turned around and saw Jesus standing there, but she did not realize that it was Jesus.

"Woman," he said, "why are you crying? Who is it you are looking for?"

Thinking he was the gardener, she said, "Sir, if you have carried him away, tell me where you have put him, and I will get him."

Jesus said to her, "Mary."

She turned toward him and cried out in Aramaic, "Rabboni!" (which means Teacher).

JOHN 20:1, 11–16

Her Character

Though mistakenly characterized as a prostitute, the Bible only says that Mary was possessed by seven demons. She probably suffered a serious mental illness from which Jesus delivered her. She is a beautiful example of a woman whose life was poured out in response to God's extravagant grace.

Her Sorrow

To watch Jesus' agony at Calvary.

Her Joy

To have been the first witness to the resurrection.

*S*he made her way through the shadows to the garden tomb, grateful for the darkness that hid her tears. How, she wondered, could the world go on as though nothing had happened?

For the last three years she had followed the rabbi. She felt privileged to tell the story of how Jesus had restored her sanity by driving out the demons that tormented her. To be close to Jesus; to witness healing after healing; to be stirred, surprised, and challenged by his teaching—this indeed was joy to one unaccustomed to joy.

But suddenly the religious leaders of Jerusalem arrested him and had him put to death.

Mary waited through the awful hours of his agony, unable to look at the spectacle before her, yet unable to turn away. However terrible the scene, she needed to be near him.

Now, as she approached the tomb to anoint his body, she wondered how she would roll away the massive stone that covered it. To her surprise the grave was already open. And empty. What had they done with his body?

She stood outside the tomb weeping. Then, bending over, she looked inside. Two creatures in white sat where the body had been laid. "Woman, why are you weeping?" they asked.

"They have taken my Lord," she said.

Then she turned and saw a man studying her.

"Woman," he said, "why are you weeping? Whom are you looking for?"

Mistaking him for the gardener, she pleaded, "Sir, if you carried him away, tell me where you laid him, and I will take him."

"Mary," Jesus said.

Mary fell to the ground in awe.

The risen Jesus appeared not to rulers and kings, nor even first of all to his male disciples, but to a woman whose love had held her at the cross and led her to the grave. Mary Magdalene, a person who had been deranged, whose testimony would not have held up in court because she was a woman, was the first witness of the Resurrection.

Blessed are those who have learned to
acclaim you,
  who walk in the light of your
presence, O LORD.
They rejoice in your name all day
long;
  they exult in your righteousness.
For you are their glory and strength. . . .

PSALM 89:15–16

When I said, "My foot is slipping,"
  your love, O LORD, supported me.
When anxiety was great within me,
  your consolation brought joy to
my soul.

PSALM 94:18–19

Cast all your anxiety on God
because he cares for you.

1 PETER 5:7

~For Prayer~

One day this week set your alarm clock so that you wake up just before dawn. Find a spot where you can watch the sunrise. In the early morning shadows, tell God about some area of darkness in your own life or in the life of someone you love. Perhaps it's an illness, a persistent sin, loneliness, a troubled marriage, an addiction, or a wayward child. As the sun rises, meditate on that first Easter morning and remember that when Jesus walked out of the tomb you walked out with him. Ask God for the faith to wait and watch for his delivering power.

⚓

Lord, make me a woman like Mary Magdalene, who follows you because of an overwhelming sense of gratitude and love for your extravagant grace. Help me surrender my darkness to you and flood me with the light of your presence.

⚓

Dorcas

Which is a Greek word meaning "gazelle." Its Hebrew equivalent is Tabitha.

In Joppa there was a disciple named Tabitha (which, when translated, is Dorcas), who was always doing good and helping the poor. About that time she became sick and died ... so when the disciples heard that Peter was in Lydda, they sent two men to him and urged him, "Please come at once!"

Peter went with them, and when he arrived he was taken upstairs to the room. All the widows stood around him, crying and showing him the robes and other clothing that Dorcas had made while she was still with them.

Peter sent them all out of the room; then he got down on his knees and prayed. Turning toward the dead woman, he said, "Tabitha, get up." She opened her eyes, and seeing Peter she sat up. He took her by the hand and helped her to her feet. Then he called the believers and the widows and presented her to them alive.

ACTS 9:36–41

Her Character

She belonged to one of the earliest Christian congregations. She was a disciple known for her practical works of mercy.

Her Sorrow

To have suffered a grave illness.

Her Joy

To serve Jesus by serving the poor.

*T*he winds roared over the coast, piling water in noisy heaps along the rocky shoreline. But though she lay quietly in the upper room of her house near the sea, Dorcas did not hear them. Nor did she notice the waves of grief that spilled into the room from the heart of every woman present. For once she had nothing to offer, no word of comfort, no act of kindness to soften their suffering. Instead, she lay still as other women ministered to her, tenderly sponging her body clean to prepare it for burial.

As Peter approached the house, he could hear the noise of mourning, more desolate than the tearing wind. Two men had summoned him, urging him to come quickly because one of the Lord's disciples in Joppa had died. He had come in haste, hoping to reach Dorcas before she had to be buried.

As soon as he entered the room where her body lay, the widows surrounded Peter with tangible evidence of the woman they loved, weeping as they held up robes and other items she had sewn to clothe the poor.

Quickly he shooed them from the room as though to clear the atmosphere of despair. Then he knelt beside her body.

As Peter prayed, he may have recalled a startling promise Jesus had made while he was on earth: "I tell you the truth, anyone who has faith in me will do what I have been doing. He will do even greater things than these, because I am going to the Father."

His faith rising like the wind outside, Peter addressed the dead woman, "Dorcas, get up." Taking her by the hand, he actually helped her to her feet.

Though Scripture doesn't tell us how Dorcas responded to her incredible experience, it doesn't take much to imagine her joy. The story of her miracle spread throughout Joppa, leading many to believe.

Have faith in God. ... I tell you, whatever you ask for in prayer, believe that you have received it, and it will be yours.

MARK 11:22, 24

Is any one of you in trouble? He should pray. Is anyone happy? Let him sing songs of praise. Is any one of you sick? He should call the elders of the church to pray over him and anoint him with oil in the name of the Lord. And the prayer offered in faith will make the sick person well; the Lord will raise him up. If he has sinned, he will be forgiven. Therefore confess your sins to each other and pray for each other so that you may be healed. The prayer of a righteous man is powerful and effective.

JAMES 5:13–16

~ For Prayer ~

Is there a Dorcas in your life, a good woman who is suffering in some way? Someone, perhaps, who has been a great support to you? Resist the temptation to become depressed about what is happening to her and, instead, spend time this week praying in light of Dorcas's story. Let her miracle increase your faith and shape your prayers. Ask God to bring light out of the darkness of present circumstances.

Lord, show me how to pray with increasing faith, aware that your Spirit is no less powerful today than two thousand years ago. Act on behalf of your servant, and glorify your name by what you do.

Which probably signifies that she was from Lydia, a region in Asia Minor.

Luke wrote, "We traveled to Philippi, a Roman colony and the leading city of that district of Macedonia. And we stayed there several days.

On the Sabbath we went outside the city gate to the river, where we expected to find a place of prayer. We sat down and began to speak to the women who had gathered there. One of those listening was a woman named Lydia, a dealer in purple cloth from the city of Thyatira, who was a worshiper of God. The Lord opened her heart to respond to Paul's message. When she and the members of her household were baptized, she invited us to her home. 'If you consider me a believer in the Lord,' she said, 'come and stay at my house.' And she persuaded us."

ACTS 16:12–15

Her Character

A Gentile adherent of Judaism, she was a successful businesswoman who sold a type of cloth prized for its purple color. As head of her household, she may have been either widowed or single.

Her Sorrow

To see Paul and Silas beaten and thrown into prison for the sake of the gospel.

Her Joy

That God's Spirit directed Paul and his companions to Macedonia, enabling her and others at Philippi to hear the gospel for the first time.

*T*he wind rustled the branches that formed a swaying canopy over the women bowed in prayer. The river's edge had become their place of worship, a green sanctuary where they gathered each Sabbath to pray.

Lydia listened as a stranger from Tarsus invoked familiar words: "Hear, O Israel! The Lord is our God, the Lord alone!" But Paul did not stop there. Instead, he spoke of a God whose son had been murdered for love. His name was Jesus. And he had risen from the grave after suffering the most agonizing death imaginable. He was the Messiah, who had come to save God's people.

Tears rolled down Lydia's cheeks, though she felt more like singing than crying. She and her household were soon baptized in the river, and Lydia insisted that Paul and his companions accept her hospitality. A Gentile who had come to Philippi from Asia Minor, Lydia was a prominent businesswoman who sold fine cloth to those who could afford it. Her home may have become the center of the church in Philippi.

Shortly after Lydia's conversion, she heard news that Paul and Silas had been whipped and thrust into prison for the crime of driving an evil spirit from a slave girl. The girl's owners dragged Paul and Silas before the city magistrates, claiming, "These men are Jews and are disturbing our city."

After their release, Paul returned to Lydia's home for a short while. As Lydia said goodbye to the apostle and his companions, she may have remembered the words of his accusers. Paul and Silas had indeed disturbed the citizens of Philippi, throwing the city into an uproar. In fact the gospel had thrown the entire region into an uproar from which it would never recover.

Lydia was Paul's first convert in Europe and the first member of the church at Philippi, a community that later became a source of great consolation to the apostle when he was imprisoned in Rome. Perhaps her prayers, joined with those of the other women gathered at the riverbank, helped prepare the way for the gospel to be planted and take root in Europe.

*Let them give thanks to the L*ORD *for*
his unfailing love
and his wonderful deeds for men,
for he satisfies the thirsty
and fills the hungry with good things.

PSALM 107:8–9

*Speak to one another with psalms,
hymns and spiritual songs. Sing and
make music in your heart to the Lord,
always giving thanks to God the Father
for everything, in the name of our Lord
Jesus Christ.*

EPHESIANS 5:19–20

~ For Prayer ~

Try inviting a few friends to join you in a time of prayer. Gather in your home or find your own "green sanctuary" outdoors. Sing hymns and ask God for a fresh outpouring of his Spirit in your churches, homes, neighborhoods, and nation. Pray for a greater opening for the gospel. Perhaps God will create an "uproar" in your city because of your prayers.

Lord, come and dwell with us as we seek your face. Let the fresh wind of your Holy Spirit fall on us. May our churches, homes, and neighborhoods become places of prayer, shaking the world around us in a way that brings you glory.

Priscilla

Which means

"worthy" or

"venerable."

[In Corinth Paul] met a Jew named Aquila, a native of Pontus, who had recently come from Italy with his wife Priscilla, because Claudius had ordered all the Jews to leave Rome. Paul went to see them, and because he was a tentmaker as they were, he stayed and worked with them. Every Sabbath he reasoned in the synagogue, trying to persuade Jews and Greeks. ...

Apollos ... was a learned man, with a thorough knowledge of the Scriptures. He had been instructed in the way of the Lord, and he spoke with great fervor and taught about Jesus accurately, though he knew only the baptism of John. He began to speak boldly in the synagogue. When Priscilla and Aquila heard him, they invited him to their home and explained to him the way of God more adequately.

Acts 18:2–4, 24–26

Her Character

One of the first missionaries and a leader of the early church, Priscilla was a woman whose understanding of the faith helped build up the church.

Her Sorrow

To experience opposition to the gospel, from both Jews and Gentiles.

Her Joy

To spread the gospel and nurture the church.

Priscilla's faith had been planted in an atmosphere of strife and controversy, first in Rome and later in Corinth. It was a wealthy seaport, famous for its commercial might and appetite for vice, hardly a place to nurture the faith of a new believer. Yet that was where God transplanted her and her husband Aquila after Claudius expelled the Jews from Rome.

In Corinth the couple met Paul of Tarsus, a Jew who had ruthlessly persecuted Jesus' followers until his own dramatic conversion. Lately he had been traveling in Asia Minor and Macedonia, preaching the gospel. When he arrived in Corinth, he probably met the couple through their common trade as tentmakers. Priscilla and Aquila invited Paul to stay in their home and work with them. After eighteen months, Paul set sail for Ephesus, taking Priscilla and Aquila with him.

The three missionaries must have been eager to see a city that ranked in importance with Rome and Corinth. True to form, Paul's preaching soon resulted in a riot, from which he escaped with his life thanks to the wise counsel of other believers, possibly including Priscilla.

When Paul left Ephesus, Priscilla and Aquila took charge of the church that met in their home.

Before long another Jew arrived, preaching eloquently about Jesus. But Apollos had grasped only a shadow of the gospel, one more in keeping with the message of John the Baptist than of Jesus. Rather than denouncing him, Priscilla and Aquila took him aside and instructed him in the faith. They did their job so well that Apollos eventually went on to Corinth, where he advanced the work Paul had begun.

Priscilla must have been a spiritually mature woman whose gifts equipped her for leadership. Priscilla's role in instructing Apollos and leading the early church is remarkable. Her name precedes Aquila's four out of the six times they are mentioned in the New Testament, possibly signifying her greater abilities as a leader or the fact that her family hailed from a higher social strata than his. Her leadership helped the early church flourish in a culture steeped in paganism.

Who shall separate us from the love of Christ? Shall trouble or hardship or persecution or famine or nakedness or danger or sword? ...

No, in all these things we are more than conquerors through him who loved us. For I am convinced that neither death nor life, neither angels nor demons, neither the present nor the future, nor any powers, neither height nor depth, nor anything else in all creation, will be able to separate us from the love of God that is in Christ Jesus our Lord.

Romans 8:35, 37–39

So then, just as you received Christ Jesus as Lord, continue to live in him, rooted and built up in him, strengthened in the faith as you were taught, and overflowing with thankfulness.

Colossians 2:6–7

~For Prayer~

Our lives are meant to have a ripple effect, so that others may feel the influence of our gifts and faith. Snatch a quiet moment and imagine yourself as a stone in the hand of God. Watch him throw you out into the water. What kind of ripples do you see? Perhaps your brother is a Christian because you shared your faith. Maybe a child has responded to God's forgiveness because she first experienced yours. Perhaps God has used you to bring justice to a situation of great injustice. Pray that God will make waves with your faith, even rocking a few boats along the way.

Father, I don't want to settle for the status quo, professing belief in you and then acting as though everything good in life comes from the world around me. Enable me to be like Priscilla, whose faith grew despite her surroundings. Let the ripple effect of my faith build up your church.

Ann Spangler is the former editorial director and vice-president of Servant Publications. Most recently she was a senior acquisitions editor at Zondervan Publishing House. The author of the best-selling books *An Angel a Day* and *A Miracle a Day*, she lives with her two daughters in Belmont, Michigan.

Jean E. Syswerda is a former editor and associate publisher for Zondervan Bibles. While at Zondervan, she was responsible for such best-selling Bibles as the *NIV Women's Devotional Bible*, the *NIV Adventure Bible*, and the *NIV Teen Study Bible*. She and her husband have three grown children and live in Allendale, Michigan.

Prayer Through the Eyes of Women of the Bible is based on the best-selling book, *Women of the Bible* by Ann Spangler and Jean E. Syswerda. *Women of the Bible* focuses on the lives of 52 remarkable women in Scripture—women whose struggles to live with faith and courage are not unlike our own. This year-long devotional book offers a unique method to help you slow down and savor the story of God's unrelenting love for his people, offering a fresh perspective that will nourish and strengthen your relationship with him.

Women of the Bible
is available at stores everywhere
for $16.99 (hardcover).